Approximately Nowhere

MICHAEL HOFMANN

faber and faber

First published in 1999
by Faber and Faber Limited
3 Queen Square London WC1N 3AU

Photoset by Wilmaset Ltd, Birkenhead, Wirral
Printed in England by Mackays of Chatham plc, Chatham, Kent

A CIP record for this book
is available from the British Library

ISBN 0–571–19524–5

1001587599

T

10 9 8 7 6 5 4 3 2 1

for L.

'When the trees were there I cared that they were there, and now they are gone.'

Paul Bowles

Contents

PART THREE

Acknowledgements

After Ovid: New Metamorphoses (co-edited with James Lasdun, Faber, 1994), *Antaeus: the Final Issue, Den Blå Port, Columbia, The Forward Book of Poetry 1996, Grand Street, Kris, Leave to Stay* (Virago), *London Magazine, London Review of Books, New Writing 4, 5, 6, 7* and *8* (Vintage), *The Observer, A Parcel of Poems* (for Ted Hughes), *Pequod, PN Review, Poetry Review, Poetry Wales, The Ring of Words, Thumbscrew, Times Literary Supplement.*

'For Gert Hofmann, died 1 July 1993' was printed in a limited edition and parallel text by de lange Afstand, Zutphen, Holland.

'Last Walk', 'Zirbelstraße', 'Metempsychosis', 'Fairy Tale', 'Abscission' and 'Near Hunstanton' appeared in *The New Yorker*.

The poems for my father were broadcast in a Radio 3 series produced by Tim Dee.

I am indebted to the Arts Council of England for a Writer's Bursary which helped me complete this book.

M.H.

Tea for My Father

I think of his characteristic way
of saying 'tea', with his teeth
bared and clenched in anticipation.
It is not his first language nor
his favourite drink, so there is
something exotic about both word and
thing. He asks for it several times
a day, in the morning and afternoon
only. Mostly it is to help him work.
He likes it very strong, with cream,
in mugs, and sweetens it himself.
He puts it on the window-sill in front
of his table, and lets it go cold.
Later on, I come and throw it out.

(*1979*)

PART ONE

v

For Gert Hofmann, died 1 July 1993

The window atilt, the blinds at half-mast,
the straw star swinging in the draught, and my father
for once not at his post, not in the penumbra
frowning up from his manuscript at the world.

Water comes running to the kitchen to separate
the lettuce for supper from the greenflies who lived there.
The sill clock ticks from its quartz heart, the everlasting radio
has its antenna bent where it pinked his eye once.

Ink, tincture of bees, the chair for him,
the chair for my mother, the white wastepaper basket
empty and abraded by so much balled-up paper,
nosebleeds and peach-pits.

The same books as for years, the only additions by himself,
an African mask over the door to keep out evil spirits,
a seventeenth-century genre scene – the children
little adults – varnished almost to blackness.

Outside, the onetime pond packed with nettles,
the cut-down-we-stand of bamboo, the berries
on the mountain ash already orange and reddening,
    although
the inscrutable blackbirds will scorn them months more.

What Happens

Blood heat at the place of the bleeding, base
of the skull, a new scowling set to my mouth,
scattiness, contempt, emulousness, laughter,
the hysterical use of the present tense.

Directions

The new   south east cemetery
is approximately   nowhere
ten stops by underground   then bus
zigzagging   through the suburbs
as bad as Dachau   and you end up
still getting out   a stop early
at the old   south east cemetery
on which it abuts   tenements
market gardens expressways   and then
it's huge   carp in the ponds gardeners
drunks rolling on the paths   fighting
lavender and roses   round the corner
is a café   with an upstairs
long long tables   and slabs of cake

Last Walk

The two of you, thirty-seven years married,
and only to one another, I should add –

some odd stone or metal for that, or medal –
arm in arm, old, stable (your new trick,

except at your age you don't learn new tricks,
more as if all your lives you'd understudied

age and stability), me buzzing round you
like an electron, first one side then the other,

the long walk by the concrete-bedded river,
the Sempt, whose tributaries arrive in pipes,

the heavy July whiff of river and linden,
low water, weeds, a few fish,

the ducks beside themselves at nightfall,
the unfailingly noisy dog and cherished for it,

the last remaining farm in the new suburb,
alteingesessen, a hayfield among garden plots,

all the way up to the quarry pool,
the gigantic activity of the new airport

racing day and night to completion like a new book,
and somewhere in it all, your tenderness

for a firefly.

Endstation, Erding

And the walk the other way, right out of the front door,
hat and wife and dark glasses – never now wifeless –
to shop in Kaiser's general store in the *lange Zeile*

(*calle*, *ulice*) with the battered, supposedly
indestructible maroon and yellow nylon shoulder bag,
a kind of compendious ribbon, a hand-held trawl net . . .

Shopping, like most everything, the opposite
of what it was once, economies now, bargains,
a rough and ready diet for high blood and diabetes,

but he took the same pleasure in it, bruised bananas,
knocked down but *tadellos* inside, weathered bread,
and still the old ungovernable flair for luxury,

weißt du noch, Krimsekt. Always happy shopping,
something in prospect, something to talk about,
a rest from the silvered goldfishbowl of consciousness . . .

The walk through the deserted postmodern forum
of cobbles and fountains, past the credit-happy bank,
the jink through the local newspaper office,

the library after a week taking down its display of novels
and its card *In Gedenken an Gert Hofmann†*,
the railway signals still up with the line long gone.

Epithanaton

Last words? Probably not, or none that I knew of,
by the sea with your grandsons in another country
when it happened. A completed manuscript on your desk,

and some months before, a choleric note dashed off to me
cutting me off, it would once have been said,
for nothing I could this time see that I'd done wrong,

part of your *Krankheitsbild*, I suppose, an apoplectic symptom,
so that I felt injured for once, and on the side of the angels.
A tantrum, I thought, tenderly, pityingly, *kleiner Papa*.

But nothing articulate, grandiose, bogus and spoken,
no Victor Hugo or Henry James, no *Je vois une lumière noire*
or *Ah, the distinguished thing*. When I was fifteen,

I told you about the Grateful Dead, and you liked that,
even tried it out in German, where it sounded, predictably,
a little swollen and implausible, *die dankbaren Toten*.

You looked, James might have put it, not ungrateful yourself.
Mildly bitter, thinner, wonderful actually
(I'm thinking of *deadish*, an old beer adjective),

Russian, bearded, still more sharpness about the nose
as the Russian (Tolstoy or Dostoevsky, ask Steiner) writes.
Dead, as you'd lived – more power to your elbow –

in a short-sleeved shirt. This one pink and still pretty good
(I'm afraid there were none of your clothes that I wanted any
     more,
not since I got too big for your purple-lined boots in 1971).

You were well-nigh inaccessible behind a screen
of potted yews that I had to barge through to reach you.
Sprays of pluperfect flowers at your head,

the swanky brass tag at your feet, Dr Gert Hofmann,
for your work on Henry James, a pleasingly unintimidating
effort that came to light in your papers later.

We all wanted to bring you things, give you things,
leave you things – to go with you in some form, I suppose.
A plastic ivory elephant from my sister,

who mussed up your hair each time they drove a part
     through it,
a few crumbs of lavender from me. All of it removed.
A custodian (one of your characters,

morbid and fussy and phlegmatic) took out the alarmingly
     long screws
from the coffin, as though someone would try very hard
to get out or – you would have said – in,

and first stood there holding the lid, then on my appeal,
took it off and himself with it. I hardly dared touch you,
your empty open hands on the awful mendacious coverlet,

the ochre bodystocking pancake colour of you,
and then fearfully the base of my thumb grazed your hand,
you cold who all my life had been a volcano.

After the funeral music – brass I asked for,
probably wrongly – we said our *Lebwohl* to you,
the inappropriate expression hurt as much as anything.

Like a cavalier swain, I speared my flowers at my feet,
a no-throw, the *blaue Blume* of the Romantics, delphiniums,
blue for faith, and turned on my heel,

prematurely, unconscionably, leaving you behind.
Then, while my back was turned, you went up in smoke,
more *dicke Luft*.

Beatitudes

I think he must have foreseen everything, even this:
his name, 'Dr Gert Hofmann' – mortuary punctilio! –
in brass, himself tipped up in a medium coffin,

a mite of disgust on his face
while the other side of the plate glass two children,
window-shopping, gawp at their first corpse.

There wasn't, as he discovered, a career in it,
but he never underestimated the morbidity of children.
To his future in-laws as a young man

he 'lacked innocence'. (Strange requirement:
innocence of the young!) To my mother he proposed
an association against marriage. Later he proposed.

It was Chekhov who said where there are too many cures
the patient must reckon with the worst
– death not cure.

And so he foresaw the pages of strenuous doctor's prose
(lacking innocence, I would say) the doctors
wrote my mother when he died.

He foresaw his car unhoused and on the street,
while the doctor moving in garages his own.
The doctor stretching his patience, displaying

consideration, while his overbearing children play,
look out powerpoints for their televisions, itching
to tear down the bookshelves and inherit the earth.

Zirbelstraße

for my mother, and in memory of my father

She's moving out of the house now, the sticky sycamores
one after the other struck by lightning outside the picture
    window
that my father struck by lightning liked to keep curtained
before the lightning came for him a second time early one
    morning
and he lost his balance, his speech, and last of all his mischief,

the high pines that gave the street its name chopped down
by the new people, only the birches left standing
whose thin leaves and catkins reminded me of her copper
    silver hair,
the old woman upstairs with all her marbles and mobility
put in a home by her Regan of a daughter who sold the house

over the heads of my parents, sitting-duck tenants,
bourgeois gypsies, wheeled suitcases on top of fitted wardrobes,
the windows where my sister's criminal boyfriends climbed in
    at night,
over the hedge the pool where the dentist's children screamed,
the old couple next door, *Duzfreunde* of Franz Josef Strauß,

the patio stones with their ineradicable growths of moss,
the weedy lawn where slugs set sail of an evening and met
    their ends
like Magellan, sliced up in the salty shallows of their own
    froth,
the potatoes my father bestirred himself to grow one year,
gravelly bullets too diamond hard to take a fork,

moving with all the books, the doubtful assets of a lifetime,
the steel table only I had the wit to assemble and left my feet on,
the furniture and lamps picked up in border raids to Italy,
once austerely challenging, now out-of-date *moderne*,
too gloomy to read by, and sad as anything not bought old,

the Strindberg kitchen with the dribbling Yugoslav fridge,
the Meissen collection we disliked and weren't allowed to use,
the démodé gadgets for making yoghurt, for Turkish coffee,
the turkey cutlets not so much cooked as made safe in the
	frying pan,
the more cooking cut corners and dwindled and became
	rehash,

my off-and-on kingdom in the cellar, among the skis and old
	boots,
my father's author's copies and foreign editions,
the blastproof metal doors, preserves, tin cans and board-
	games
of people who couldn't forget the Russians, the furnace room
where my jeans were baked hard against an early departure.

Still Life

A sort of overgrown phial,
opaque blown glass of the sort
we once saw them making at Murano,
whitish – with blue? with yellow?

And sticking out of it
that odd trouvaille, a dried yard
of was it hogweed, *Schweinekraut*,
Schweinswurzel, something swinish about it,

some hollow dill-like plant
withered to articulate straw
that my father half-inched,
like a spindly triffid on the steel table.

It was an artistic endeavour really,
a momentary juxtaposition
that gathered dust, languishing
like umbrella ribs in an elephant's foot,

in saecula saeculorum.
As it grew dark, he drew the curtains,
so as not to be seen, or not to show
how much he couldn't see.

There was a drawn atmosphere
as in Buñuel or *La Grande Bouffe*,
like being locked up overnight
in an impoverished modern art museum

– as it were, Beuys in Buffalo –

and we slumped like astronauts
in the too-low leather seats
while he peeled and chopped fruit
and handed it around.

de passage

From you I know we owe it to the others
to make more of an effort,

to talk to the stallholders
in something approaching their language,

to pass the time of day – all that regular guy,
homme du peuple stuff that so dismayed me –

to stand in gatherings feet crossed
like apprehensive flamingoes,

to issue oblique challenges
to senior colleagues with a shy smile,

and not to go abroad in the garden suburbs
we've temporarily lucked into

without a pair of scissors in our pockets.

Cheltenham

The nouveau oil building
spoils the old water town, spook town, old folks' town.
My old parents, like something out of Le Carré,
shuffle round the double Georgian square

tracing figures of eight, endless figures of eight,
defected ice-dance trainers or frozen old spooks,
patinage, badinage,
reminiscence with silences.

Then a family event if ever there was one:
my mother reads my translation of my father,
who hasn't read aloud since his 'event'.
Darkness falls outside. Inside too.

Ted Hughes is in the small audience,
and afterwards asks my father
whether he ever, like an Innuit,
dreamed of his own defeat and death.

My father, who's heard some questions, but never anything
like this, doesn't know Ted Hughes,
perhaps hears 'idiot', gives an indignant no
in his miraculously clear English.

More laps of the marred green,
the pink sky silts down, a November afternoon
by the clock, his last in England.
The days brutally short; a grumpy early night.

Metempsychosis

Your race run, the rest of us,
mother, sisters, sisters' boyfriends,
ran repairs. Trimmed the hedge,
whited the walls, weeded the stones.

The place looked five years younger –
you might not have recognized it.
It took you dead to harness us,
give us some common, Tolstoyan purpose.

It was the day the ants queened themselves,
or whatever they do. Got to the end,
and came back all self-conscious with silver wings,
folding stuff they hardly knew what to do with.

Like the Ossis in Berlin, they got everywhere
(a run on cuckoo clocks). The clever ones
would go far, to be in position for
the next pedestrian incarnation.

PART TWO

Essex

They turned your pet field into a country club,
and the cemetery was grey with rabbits
and the graves of your friends
who had died young, of boredom.

Fidelity

for James, again

At the old *Tramontana*
on Tottenham Court Road
among the hi-fi shops
I learned to order

what you ordered,
not studenty noodles
but sophisticated things
like the special.

After years of our
playing at lunch,
the old waiter shook himself
to death with Parkinson's

practically before our eyes.
(I remember the rattle
and slop of one last
saucerful of coffee.)

One afternoon,
when we no longer went there
like Hem to the War,
I saw Joseph Brodsky

sitting in the window
with paper and a cigarette,
the recording angel,
miles away.

Ingerlund

The fat boy by Buddha out of Boadicea
with the pebbledash acne and half-timbered haircut,
sitting on the pavement with his boots in the gutter,

we must have made his day when we pulled over
and asked him for the site of the Iron Age fort
in his conservation village.

Parerga

In the bedside drawer of a hotel room
in the black naugahyde and pigtail German Eighties,
I came upon the *Yellow Pages* and a Gideon's Bible,
one of them – which one? –
pregnant with the local chickenhawk guide.

The Station Road, the Primrose Path

To the station in my red boots in the mid-Eighties:
to London, a broken-off book review in my pocket –
in this, as in everything else (the station,
the boots, the mid-Eighties) a generation late.

Meeting you coming the other way, all of a sudden
I urgently wanted to proceed no further
than the back of the nearest bicycle shed
and there go to ground like two snails . . .

No to cerebration, no to the Spillers building
and the cachet of phoney language schools,
no to the delayed electrification of the East Coast line
and my unwritten, never-to-be-written style paragraph.

Conversation

'Too drunk to fuck or drive, the baby with its father,
my doubles brought out in two tot glasses,
some herby German swill, sweet, I like it, *digestif*, he says,

I'm drunk, I have my foot on the chair, my knee
up alongside my face, I haven't eaten for two days,
he's thinking about my legs, I tell him I'm drunk,

America is a cesspool, I blame television,
then I all but empty my pack of Camels into my glass,
he takes a wet cigarette and lights it from my lighter,

I knock over my second tot glass and it puddles on the table,
he's talking but I can't understand the half of it,
though he has a poem that has "forever England" in it,

and I tell him I like that, well, it's probably enough anyway,
then I suddenly feel very quiet, he's asking me
about my writing and I lean forward and puke.'

Vecchi Versi

It's just abstract, you say: when I'm not here,
I don't exist and my perspectives are warped.
Nostalgia, the bloom of recollection –
a false spring . . . You can't run your life
by these conceits like productivity agreements.

. . . It's a holiday of some sort.
The music on the radio is for kissing.
You go to visit your thin-lipped friend,
who happens to be a musician himself.

You drink wine and sit at a table
and talk. Some things you talk around.
Then you are on the same side of the table.
He has some Durex, you let him fuck you.
– He was kind of lonesome, as the words go.

(*1980*)

Intimations of Immortality

Have a nice day and get one free –
this is retirement country,
where little old ladies

squinny over their dashboards
and bimble into the millennium,
with cryogenics to follow;

the shuttle astronauts
hope to fluff re-entry and steal
one last record-breaking orbit;

where they give a man
five death sentences
to run more or less concurrently.

I take turns in my three chairs,
and try to remember two switches for lights,
the third for waste.

My eyes sting from salt and sun-oil,
and I drink orange juice
till it fizzes and after.

The sight of a cardinal
or the English Sundays on Thursday
makes it a red letter day.

Lizards flirt in the swordgrass,
grasshoppers bow their thighs
at six sharp, and quite suddenly,

after seventy-five years,
the laurel oak crashes out.
See you later, if not before.

(*Gainesville*)

Kleist in Paris

Dearest Mina,

                thank you for yours, my first news
of you in ten weeks. Imagine my happiness
when I saw my address in your handwriting.
But then the postmaster wanted to see my passport,
and I didn't have it on me. I begged him
to make an exception, swore that I was Kleist,
but it was in vain. Deceived a thousand times,
he couldn't believe there was an honest man
left in Paris. I went home to get my passport,
and read your letter in a café, quite exhausted.
You are so earnest. Despite all the trouble
I cause you, you still manage to be cheerful.
It moved me so much that I left the theatre
where I was waiting to see a great play,
and ran out to answer you with enthusiasm.
– You want me to tell you about my spirit?
Willingly. The storm has settled somewhat,
the sailor feels the gentle, swelling motion
that announces a bright and sunny day.
Perhaps I can even bless this stay in Paris.
Not for its sparse joys, but because it has
taught me that knowledge leads to immorality.
The most developed nation is ready to decline.
When I see the works of Rousseau and Voltaire
in libraries, I think: what is the point?
Why does the state subsidise education?
Love of truth? The state?! A state only thinks
about getting a return on its investment.
It wants comfort, luxury and sophistication.

What can transcend chicken *à la suprême*?
But man is drawn irresistibly to the sciences.
He rolls the wheel of fire up the mountainside,
and shoulders it again when it reaches bottom.
If progress doesn't accomplish happiness,
should we say no to it? Forget what we know?
The alternative to decadence is superstition.
Where brightness exists, there is also shadow ...
When you consider that it takes a lifetime
to learn how to live, that on our deathbed
we still don't know what Heaven demands,
how can God expect responsibility from Man?
And don't let anyone talk of a 'quiet inner voice'.
The same voice that calls upon the Christian
to forgive his enemy, instructs the savage
to roast him, and he eats him up with reverence
in his heart. What then is Evil? The things
of this world are ramified in thousands of ways,
every deed is the mother of a million others,
and often the best is sired by the worst.
Whatever anyone says about Attila and Nero,
the Huns, the Crusades and the Inquisition,
still this friendly planet rolls through space,
spring comes round again, and people live,
enjoy themselves and die, just as always ...
Freedom, my own house, and a wife, I pray
for these every day, my three monastic vows.
Heaven's promised gift to Man is *joie de vivre*.
Man has to work for it by doing good on earth.
I haven't made up my mind what to do yet.
Writing is for ever, so I won't commit myself
any further. Be patient and hope for the best.
And don't let a day pass without seeing me.

You can find me in the shady part of the garden,
or upstairs in Carl's room, or by the stream
that flows from the lime-trees into the Oder.
May the past and the future sweeten your present,
may you be happy as in a dream, until – well,
who could spell it out? A long kiss on your lips.

P.S. Greet your parents from me – tell me,
why do I feel uneasy whenever I think of them,
and never of you? It is because you understand me.
I wish the whole world could see into my heart!
Yes, greet them, say that I honour them,
whatever their opinion of me. Write soon –
no longer *poste restante*, but Rue Noyer 21.

(*1982*)

Rimbaud on the Hudson

Some kill somewhere upstate. Bud light,
a gutted mill, three storeys of brickwork,
mattresses and condoms, elder and sumac,
child abusers fishing for chub in heavy water.

Masque

> 'Brother, fall you back a little
> With the bony lady.' – Tourneur

The government is fucking a corpse.
It doesn't have an erection, but it's fucking a corpse.

Sweat is beading on its brow. 'Come on,'
it says, 'won't you love me just a little bit.'

The government is fucking a corpse. It has eight arms,
or perhaps there are several of them doing it.

They are waving toy bombs and toy vibrators and toy money
and toy cars and toy whips and a toy bottle of HP sauce

and a toy money-back guarantee. The government
is fucking a corpse. The corpse is for real.

(1994)

Scylla and Minos

I knew about Helen, they kept selling me Helen,
but I never even got to be stolen in the first place.
Sieges are boring – did you know. Everything's fine,
just each day's a little bit worse than the last.

And you start thinking how long it is since you saw
prawns or a nice pair of earrings or a magazine.
I had my townhouse, but I practically lived on the battlements,
they even let me use the telescope during the lulls.

Then one day I saw him. That changed everything.
Oiled limbs, greaves (can you imagine), his little skirt,
roaring and rampaging about, the bellowed (yes, taurean)
    commands.
By Jupiter out of Europa, apparently. I thought: gimme!

A big girl wants a man like that, not the little weasels
scurrying around defending me. (Did I ask to be defended?)
I started cheering him on as he skewered our guys.
I wondered if he could see me and what he thought.

Was he stuffing a goat, hitting the 3 star, or letters home?
Minos, Minos King of Crete. I tried on a Cretan accent,
did that all the hair up all the hair down thing they do there.
I thought of the word Argive – or were we the Argives?

Perhaps if we lost – and how could we fail to lose,
how could anyone hold out against him, he's so irresistible –
then I'd get to be his wife or his sex slave or something.
Who cares, frankly. Isn't that what happens. After a war?

[37]

That's when I started thinking about trying to help things
along.
Not pushing 'our boys' over the edge, or distracting them
from the job in hand
by giving them blow jobs as they manned the walls (man
something else),
something more ruthless, I suppose, and more wholesale.

I wrote to Minos, signed 'a fan', to meet me at the gate.
It wasn't easy, believe me. At night I spiked their drinks.
I went into Daddy's bedroom with the garden shears
and cut off his purple scalplock. The creepy thing went and
bled on me.

There. I shouldn't have told you. Anyway, I popped it in a bag
and ran to the Maidens' Gate. He wasn't there of course.
So I had to pick my way through his dreaming army
with it in my hands, by now it was hissing softly.

He was up, of course (so conscientious!),
in something skimpy, bustling about his tent,
wet jockstraps hanging up to dry. (What I'd give!)
The funny thing is he didn't seem pleased to see me, I looked.

I said: This is the purple hair of Nisus.
The siege is over. Invest the town. (Invest me!)
He got all huffy, gave me stuff about war and men and honour,
said something so underhand had no place in the annals, etc.,

and no way was I ever going to Crete at his side.
I said did he like war so much, he didn't want it to end.
The next day his flag was flying over Megara
and they were loading the ships.

He dictated peace terms. My father abdicated.
I stumbled about the campsite, thinking what I'd done,
what there was for me to do. I couldn't go back,
and which of the other towns on the strip would have me –

like giving houseroom to the Trojan horse,
the Trojan bicycle more like. It was Crete or nothing.
He stood by the mast, arms crossed, for all the world like
    Ulysses.
I said: Fuck you, Minos, your wife does it with bulls!

Then I saw my father coming for me, he was an osprey,
he was rejuvenated, I gave a little mew of terror,
and found myself flying too, criss-crossing the sea,
Scylla the scissor-legged, now the shearer.

The Log of Meleager's Life

The woman who gave you life, put her hand,
her whole body, into the fire for you,
pulled you out, red-blue, bald and blistered,
remembers the agony with every candle on your cake –
what if she'd the right to return you
to non-being for something you'd said or done,
or just calling in a debt, to stand there
at either end of your life like Kafka's doorman,
judge and jury, while you burn (baby) in ignorance?

Hotel New York, Rotterdam

for Joachim Sartorius

Clouds, oil barges and airliners blow down the Maas,
chimneys, cranes and warships stay where they are,
the Hotel – you should be so lucky – New York
stays where it is, half church, half castle,
on its headland or island, fork or confluence,
where emigrants camped out in the Thirties,

watching the river, the schedules, the post, each other,
the great clock and the smaller one with the cardinal points,
the clipper ship weathervane, the tubby warehouses,
taking it in turns to eat and sleep and talk,
the wind blowing the money out of their pockets,
their morale out of the window, their lives into a flat spin.

One Line for Each Year of Life

i.m. Joseph Brodsky

A window that won't . . . the campus flag (your *drap/drapeau*)
and a muddle of pale or liver-coloured buildings.
I'm like a cosmonaut-understudy-cum-*Gastarbeiter*.
At the sound of a pneumatic drill or steam-hose

I make my way to East Engineering and begin to teach.
My neighbours here are cars on the open top deck
of multi-storey car-parks, while the many elevators
have made me somewhat weak at the knee.

One day there was A/C, the next heating.
It's called fall. Holsum bread vans.
Armoured cars carrying snacks and sweats.
Beer trucks (lite, worse luck) as long as tankers.

Beggars in doorways have 'Image Consultants'
on their plastic bags. Youths in outsize trousers
skateboard over the car-park, jump off a ramp
and try to hit the ground in one piece.

(You know the feeling.) Grackles or jackdaws
roost in the near-dark, fly up and come down,
black on black. There's a sponsored squirrel,
you might think, for every student. Or vice versa.

Books on the floor, stubs in the lid of a jam-jar.
Cups used for a week, hot and cold, plates ditto.
(Quentin Crisp at least used to turn his over.)
The room is ivory, like an *Altbau* igloo.

This is where you dreamed of your name on an arriving letter.
I watch cars fill up their lanes and go on green.
The Christmas lights go up on State Street.
The lit sidewalk is the colour of old snow.

The yards are down to dirt and hickory nuts,
the last of the beans have clattered off the catalpa,
rubbish blows wildly on Thanksgiving,
down streets empty 'as after a nuclear strike'.

From a canal fish are swept down a slide into the Huron,
and a canny heron (rhyme?) stands by and snaps them up,
still stunned. The clock strikes (the one that Frost
described), and a flock of starlings abruptly

quit the clock tower. How many lives is a man allowed?

(Ann Arbor)

My Life and Loves

Frank Harris. And a syringe for afters.

PART THREE

Gone

for Jamie McKendrick

The usual roses on the dado, the curtain, the bedspread
and the oriental picture with cranes,
clashing with the usual magnolia on the walls . . .

The television swings into the room on a hinged extension
like a box camera or a boxing glove
or something at the dentist's.

The radio and Teasmaid are perched on shooting sticks,
the two-handled diamanté neon bedside lamp
is an apple of discord – all mine!

An hour's sleep on the back of eight hours of drink.
From the street comes the *beep beep* of Green Goddesses
    reversing.
Two suns appear in the mitred window.

Vagary

I can really only feign disapproval
of my youngest
dibbling his semolina'd fingers
in the satiny lining of her red coat.

The Adulterer

Is there martial law where you are,
a curfew, state of emergency,
suspension of civil rights?
Are there expensive German
water-cannon cruising the streets
like fast white elephants,
and are the police out in force
with their long Mr Whippy truncheons?

Are post and telecommunications
interrupted, foreign broadcasts jammed,
foreign embassies cordoned off?
Is it solemn music and wooden generals
on the airwaves? Have they sealed
the borders and must the nation
now pull together, troop movements
in the mountains, and all leave cancelled?

What happened to the poems fluttering
on the lamp-posts? Do strangers
no longer stop and chat in the streets?
Is the populace sitting at home,
cowed and angry, counting their stocks
of canned food and the dollar bills
in their socks? Are you staring hopelessly
at your children and the television?

June

Short forms. Lines, sentences, *bonmots*.
Part of an afternoon, a truncated night,
interstitial evening. Rarely a paragraph
or stanza ('room'), never a day and a day and a day...
Half-pints and double-deckers, the river, the cemetery,
always on the *qui vive* (why, ourselves of course!) –
our honeymoon epic in illicit instalments.

Megrim

Corners of the linden yellow like grapes . . .
back in July leaves blew. Rain wounds the window,
preoccupies the drainpipes, nourishes –
after a seemly interval – the mould spots
in the cornices. Stray nooses of wisteria
toss purposefully, aimlessly, who can say.

Finita la Commedia

At the end of our run
We put on rehearsals,
And it all goes swimmingly.

Near Hunstanton

These are my own crows in a mechanical flap;
my geese in ragged Vs – more Ws or Ys –
honking abysmally to one another;

my salt marsh smelling of vomit
at low tide, grown with tiny plants
the colour of rust; my oak leaves

imitating rain with their eczematic rustle;
my stone-scabbed beach impounded
peu à peu by the sea; my soft low cliffs

crumbling their beach-huts to the Northeaster;
my big skies you can see coming a mile away;
my jellyfish that you trod on in your sensible shoes.

Is It Decided

Planetary weather. A glittering
canopy of gas, otherwise not a cloud.
The sweet creep of green this English summer.
Trees addled by heat and monoxide
put out panic shoots they probably can't afford,
that then again might be the future.
I get out of breath walking twenty minutes
to the bank to draw money,
new spicy beef-and-tomato fifties.
I'm in mourning for my life —

                    or ours; or ours?

Mayakovsky

When all the other synchronized swimmers
have gone home, taking their waterproof smiles
and their webbed fingers and their nose plugs
with them, I remain behind,

holding my foot in my hand like a cramp,
like a stubble-headed clown trodden on by an elephant,
the last of the synchronized swimmers (O Osip, O Lily!),
twisting in the wind.

Seele im Raum

I could probably
just about have swung a cat
in that glory-hole –

maybe a Manx cat
or that Cheshire's gappy grin –
and for a fact I could open the door

and perhaps even the window
without raising myself
off the plumbed-in sofa

but what really hurt
was the rugby football
deflating from lack of use,

a pair of void calendars
and the pattern of my evenings
alone on the slope

overlooking the playground
the paddling pool
gradually drained of children

the bullying park attendant
crows sipping from beercans
as if they'd read Aesop,

sun gone, a nip in the air,
the grass purpling
and cold to the touch,

and later on, in near darkness,
watching a man's two boomerangs
materialize behind him

out of the gloom,
like the corners of his coffin
on leading-strings.

XXXX

for Larry Joseph

'que lo único que hace es componerse
de dias;
que es lóbrego mamífero y se peina . . .' – Vallejo

I piss in bottles,
collect cigarette ash in the hollow of my hand,
throw the ends out of the window
or douse them in the sink.

I chew longlife food,
dried fruit, pumpernickel, beef jerky.
I'm forty. I free the jammed light-push with my fingernails
to give the hall a rest.

With one stockinged foot – scrupulous pedantry –
I nudge back the loose stair-carpet on the eleventh step.
Later I might slam some doors
and spend a wet evening under a tree.

I've identified with a yellowish fox beside the railway line,
followed silent firework displays on the Thames,
seen two shooting stars burn out over London
and made wishes on them.

I can't remember when I last wrote a letter
or picked up the telephone. My smile
goes on shopkeepers and bus drivers and young mothers.
It dazzles me.

I think continually about money, and the moths eat my clothes:
the thing about earthly treasures was true.
For half an hour, amid palpitations, I watched
two children I was sure were mine.

Most of the day I'm either lying down
or asleep. I haven't read this many books
this avidly since I was a boy.
Nights are difficult. Sometimes I shout.

I'm quarrelsome, charming, lustful, inconsolable, broken.
I have the radio on as much as ever my father did,
carrying it with me from room to room.
I like its level talk.

Malvern Road

It's only a short walk, and we'll never make it,
the street where we first set up house –
set up maisonette – together . . . do you remember
the grim Tuesday *Guardian* Society-section aspect of it,
the crumbly terrace on one side,
then the road, modern and daunting but somehow in truce,

and the high-rises and multi-storey garages opposite
that gave us our view, and in winter,
like a periscope five miles away due south,
the GPO tower obliterated by Paddington Rec the rest of the
time,
and that was the only way to go from where we were,
'barely perched on the outer rim of the hub of decency',

probably we were happy but in any case
we were beyond dreams in the strange actualness of
everything,
a tyro salary, a baby mortgage, such heartstopping fun,
the place too intimate and new and connected to us
for us to think of 'entertaining'
and we liked the stairs best of everything anyway,

the *ancien* lino kitchen
where I cooked out of *The Pauper's Cookbook*
– 'a wealth, or should it be, a poverty of recipes' –
the bedroom barely wide enough to take our bed crosswise,
so we lay next to the window, the window making a third,
the creased cardboard blind bleaching like jeans,

everything cheap and cheerful,
your jaunty primary touches everywhere, fauve and mingled,
my room a grave navy ('Trafalgar') with my vast desk
like an aircraft carrier that I had to saw the legs off
to get upstairs, and then fitted the stumps on casters
so when I wrote it rolled,

the muso downstairs and on the ground floor
the night cook with a farouche squint,
his placid Spanish wife and their little Sahara,
how frightening everything was,
and with how much faith, effort and heart
we went out to meet it anyway,

the corner pub we probably never set foot in,
the health centre padlocked and grilled like an offie,
the prefab post office set down at an odd angle,
the bank that closed down, the undertaker who stayed open,
the idealistic delicatessen before God and Thatcher created
    the zuppie,
the tremulous restaurant my best friend proposed in,

the sun breeding life from dirt like Camus,
the pepper-fruited scrawny alder with two yellow days of
    pollen,
the nights of your recurring dream
where you whimpered comfort to your phantom baby boy
you didn't have and said you'd mind him, as now,
to my shame, you have and you do.

Abscission

A leaf must be a numbered, strenuous thing
to a young tree like a toe or a tooth.
But fall comes anyway to the plant nursery,
they stand there in their ornamental deaths,

the toddlers, their psychohistories, morbologies,
tipping from jelly to wax to oil-paint to human tissue.
I spectate at my defeat, feet on the dash,
smoking, leaning away, half-detached.

Lewis Hollow Road

The walls – sloping like a tent's – of pre-slathered plasterboard
depending from a single great beam, the slushy track outside
  a bobsleigh run
negotiated by the neighbours' four-wheel drives at odd hours,
the black metamorphic bulk of the treetrunk through the
  night,
icicles dripping and growing and shrinking and forking like
  Tirpitz's beard,

the outside in in the form of quills and feathers and stingray
  bones and pine cones,
Indian burial chamber bric-à-brac, the six-foot rattler in the
  mudroom,
a Spanish guitar and a Dustbuster hanging together like a
  yellow-grey Braque,
the alphabetical books at rest on many shelves and the
  unsleeping regard
of Auden and Burroughs on postcards, the sacred monsters of
  the place,

gods of incompatible religions, ourselves under a couple of
  blankets,
one of them notionally electric, sometimes knotted together
  in brief sleep,
as often each hugging his edge of the bed, lying three or four
  bodies apart,
wrestling with ourselves and our doubts and miseries, and
  you asking,
awkwardly, unexpectedly, apropos of nothing much: 'Do you
  think I'm real?'

Fou Rire

Sunday you're away
in your factor 25 sunblock,
seeing a film about ghosts.

There's a parp of brass
from the Heath,
I look through photographs,

find the missing funnybone
from the excruciating doctor game,
think of the Ahlbergs' joke:

Q: What goes ha ha bonk?
A: A man laughing his head off.
Here's Richard Gerstl's

'Self-Portrait, Laughing',
a round spinning top of a head
and a wedge for a mouth.

He was teaching the Schoenbergs
how to paint ('The Red Stare'),
ran away with the composer's wife

until friends talked her
into returning to her children
and he topped himself.

I think about it myself most days,
like my friend Ivy, who forswore shoes,
got into primal therapy,

Camus, self-mutilation,
as touchingly permeable to ideas
as a cell to a chemical –

although I'm unsure
of the scale of these things –
considered good enough once

to be a fourth-division goalkeeper,
a swimmer until he took up
Capstan full strength.

And so life becomes
a shoebox full of snaps,
though what can a chance point

say about a curve,
the pictures of you
in your various incarnations,

your ex
flexing his muscles,
or just lately me

swinging you up in the air (bloomers!),
my face lurching, crazy,
dark with blood and sun,

a magenta giant like my father,
or again Gerstl, the other hope
(after Kokoschka, who lived for ever)

of Austrian painting,
dead at maybe twenty-five, his head an orange
spiked on the clove of his neck,

more shocking than Van Gogh,
sun flecks of paint,
a silent bray of disseverance.

Fairy Tale

'and smoke too many cigarettes
and love you so much' – Frank O'Hara

It was blowing hot and cold as I sat in the window seat
in a northern town, the heating on in June,
the window sash propped open on a splint of wood
like a tired eye on a matchstick . . .

There was a sign, Thank you for not smoking,
but I didn't want thanks, I wanted to smoke.
I was living on air, cigarettes, pull-ups and kisses –
puffing away in a daze of longing.

Outside was the delicate viaduct, a redoubt,
a pair of magpies mating. The sun shone,
and there was such a fine rain falling,
no rainbow was required.

It struck me I was exactly the person
to write the life of the pink shopping bag
hovering irresolutely
on the triangular intersection below.

It's puzzling how things happen. For years,
the princess lies in the glass coffin of her life,
then fruit on her tongue, and beer,
and salt, your salt.

Gomorrah

'e l'inferno è certo' – Montale

The queer cemetery
torsos jacent on tombstones
old-fashioned looks

no conversation
not about muscles
or gyms or tans

as comforting
in its blithe transgressiveness
as a stolen baked potato

and you and I
hand in hand
looking for shade

and an untenanted
patch of grass
close to the railway line

with the new stand
at Stamford Bridge
going up behind us

or again
on top of the hill at night
in the killing heat

[68]

kein Lüftchen weht
the view of Canary Wharf
and a fizzy orange-purple sky

and at our feet the park police van
tracking an athlete
round the cinder track

surrounded by a heavenly host
twitting and outwith
guarding our guardians.

Summary

'For months the heat of love has kept me marching' – Robert Lowell

I snap my boy's bow
in the morning, wash his stiffy at night, blow my brains out
with music, anything from 'Ballade von der sexuellen
    Hörigkeit'
to 'Sexual Healing'. *Je te veux*.

*

The vaunted sod
under my feet is rolled up like a piece of turf or a blanket
in my grenadier's knapsack, along with a toothbrush
and near-pristine candle end.

*

A loose cannon
combing the phone book and the small ads for friendly
    addresses,
a nine-year-old regaling my parents with the Roget's
entry on sex. 'Anyone for urolagnia?'

*

Pulling on the telephone
like a bottle, a permanent unendurable fluttering in the
    diaphragm,
dogdays, the sighs of the Pléiade, planets in love,
mouthsounds, genie, come . . .

*

Hyde Park
twenty-four hours apart, Baker Street from the top of a bus,
the curve of the overground train past your house,
past mine, nowhere to grip in the slippery city.

    *

The London plane tree by my window
hangs its green leatherette sleeves, exhausted by a hard May.
My varsity jacket. The sky between leaves is the brightest
    thing in nature,
Virginia Woolf told the inquiring Rupert Brooke. Whatever.

Fucking

A zero sum game, our extravagant happiness,
matched or cancelled
by the equal and opposite unhappiness of others,

but who was counting as you came walking from your car,
not off the bus,
early for once, almost violent in your severity,

both of us low on our last, stolen day for a month,
uncertain, rather formal,
a day of headaches, peaches and carbonated water,

by the stone pond whose ice you smashed as a girl . . .
or how we wound up
jubilant, a seesaw at rest, not one foot on the floor.

et prope et procul

You sleep in a nest of my dirty shirts,
while, five or six time zones adrift of you
and in temperatures close to blood heat, I keep my balls
coddled in your second-best lace panties
for the duration.

Night Train

In the half-compartment
set aside for the handicapped
I crossed my feet on the battered
fire-extinguisher,

the grandfather, maybe,
of my shaken can of County
foaming at the widget,

and sat remembering the dowdily
glaring train back from Guildford,
feeling parched and let down
after our reading,

the series of benighted stops
where no one got on
– much less got off –

at one of which, at least,
I put it to you, not joking,
though you weren't to know that then,
that we might elope together

somewhere in Wild West Surrey,
wo sich die Füchse gute Nacht sagen,
before we could reach

Suburbiton and Esher
Welcomes Careful Drivers,
the sporting meccas
of Wimbledon and Twickers,

the windows of the jolly poly
where you worked behind the bar
in a thriftstore bronze dress

and short back and sides,
chronically undecided
between Venus Pandemos
and Jeanne d'Arc.

Litany

for Robin Robertson

Dear god,
           let me remember these months of transition
in a room on the Harrow Road, the traffic
muffled by a plastic sheet, the facing ziggurats
with their satellite dishes and tea-towels out to dry,
a lengthwise Brazilian flag curtaining one window,

indigents and fellow aliens and oddballs in the street,
the wobbly eyes I mistakenly looked into, wobbly and then
suddenly murderous, the fat friendly ladies and truanting
    children,
West Indian barbers and Lebanese grocers eating on the job,
the line of a hundred people outside the post office
at a minute to nine on Monday morning,

the pallet, table and two chairs
in the room at the top of the sharp and loose coir staircase,
a kettle and ashtray before I remembered about food,
the streetlamp almost within reach to slide down, fireman-
    style,
im Falle eines Falles,
the reflections of car windscreens bouncing on the ceiling,

the solicitous Irish landlady, Marie's sister, saying
'Are you alright? Now are you sure you're alright?'
the canal at the back, seedy as Xochimilco,
the May air full of seeds, alder and plane and sycamore,
generative fluff, myself fluffy and generative,
wild-haired and with the taste of L. in my mouth,

the office workers opposite
very evidently pissing behind milk-glass,
goslings and baby coots without the white stripe as yet,
attack dogs defecating on the grass,
the occasional putter of narrowboats, industrial
and bucolic as canals are industrial and bucolic,

the velvet curtains slowly turning to dust on the
    woodwormed rail,
my diminished establishment of bin-liners and suitcase
(our 1961 cardboard family 'Revelation'),
the Olympia Traveller I lugged around Mexico and two pairs
    of boots,
otherwise silence and light and dust and flies,
so hungry I picked the bin when I visited my children,

the steel doors and squats of Walterton and Elgin
from the days before pastel paint, a hulking unmistakable
    school
on the light industrial skyline, barbed wire, coupling pigeons,
yellow brick and corrugated Homebase prefab, living for
    nightfall
and the bus that took me round the houses
to heaven.